Broken Dreaı and Hope!

Andy B loves writing resources and materials to encourage and inspire!

This book is part of a series, converted from Andy B's Video Teaching Series, which you can find online at www.berrybunch.family, and search for "Broken Dreams, and Hope" or use the QR code.

The BerryBunch create digital material - to encourage and inspire families, all around the world, in their Christian faith; supporting, equipping and resourcing the Church in it's Global mission: for free, for all.

Images for Cover Artwork

www.pexels.com / www.unsplash.com / www.pixabay.com

Dedication

I have a fantastic family who have been encouraging me for so very long to believe in myself. Through some of the many twists and turns of a life worth living, I've finally put pen to paper.

I hope this encourages you, as much as my own family have encouraged me.

Thanks Olli D (otherwise known as Missionary Evangelist Olamide Dawson Adekunle). Without your effervescent joy and encouragement, I'd probably have continued to procrastinate a little longer on these writing projects.

Thankyou my darling, Jo, who is both my best friend, and my wife. You are an ever-present source of hope as I watch you never surrender your desire to become more like Jesus Christ.

Steven - your ability to say in just a few words, what I take many lines to say, is always refreshing.

Nathan – Thank you for finding such enjoyment correcting my grammar.

Peter – your joy is infectious! Nuff said!

Magdi – we miss you, but we are grateful that God let you into our lives, even for a short time. We're looking forward to meeting you again, one day, in Heaven: you beat us home!

For you, the reader of this book!

My prayer for this book is that you can find the same joy, peace, love and hope that I have found; that my family have found.

People will let us down, but God never can. That is a peace more than worth fighting for. I pray you find it!

Andy B

Foreword

Andy writes " ..But, if you're hurting, and you're broken, and you want to know a peace that isn't affected by your situation, you need to pursue God. Because God is the only true source of that peace - ..."

I have known pain...I have had Broken Dreams....we have all been hurt. The systems of this world ..and even our own humanity assures us of that. The Bible says it like this:

Job 5:7 Easy English "You know that from every fire smoke rises into the air. So every man that is born has troubles in his life."

Facing this pain and coming to terms with this reality has been very difficult for me. Extremely difficult.

In this Book my Brother and Friend helps us greatly. He lays out the facts and directs ever so gently to the source of the Peace we so desire.

I have been battered....oh yes!....and there's HOPE!

Who would have thought that the answer was spiritual? Oh. But it is!

The solution that Andy gives I tried and I have been filled with such Hope. That in spite of it all..I have Peace!..Yes ..Peace. A Peace that overflows.

I know this Author. It follows that I'm not surprised that Andy has, with sharing his heart in this book, helped me stay the course. You have been generous.

Thank you, Brother.

Olamide Dawson Adekunle – Missionary Evangelist

Yes, I am
the Vine,
you are the
branches

John 15 v 5

Contents

Introduction

A few questions to ponder...

Are you hurting inside?

Do you feel alone? Do you feel lonely, even though you're surrounded by people?

Have your emotions left you feeling tired and like you have nothing left to give?

Have you lost your job? Or a friend? Or a precious member of your family?

Are you left wondering where hope will come from?

Do you feel different from everybody around you – like you've got struggles they wouldn't and couldn't understand?

From being a victim of childhood abuse to enduring unemployment as an adult, and the tragic death of a daughter, I have lived through some pretty testing pain, but, always, God was there to walk alongside me.

And if God's plans are for our good, how can we trust that God really loves us, when bad stuff happens around us and to us?

The comforting thing is that Jesus was rejected and betrayed by one of his closest friends and companions. And while He was both Jesus and God, He still felt the pain personally, even to the point of weeping when the emotional strain overwhelmed Him.

We're all looking for something to help us feel peaceful, and we'll do it any which way we can.

But there is one certain place we can find hope. And that is in a relationship with Jesus Christ.

Chapter 1

There is an answer!

We're living in a world which is full of pain, and misery, and hurt. People are desperate for the truth, for answers, for hope.

At the time of writing, in the autumn of 2021, we are still reacting to the severity, and serious implications, of COVID-19, that turned the world upside down through 2020, into 2021, and doubtless will continue to into 2022.

We've seen people losing their jobs.

We've seen people lose loved ones.

We've seen lives defined, permanently, because people have caught COVID and come out the other side, but with what the medical community are loosely labelling as 'long COVID'.

We've seen fear and terror reign.

We've seen terrorism around the world growing, seemingly unabated and unchecked.

We've seen the terror and fear of people desperate to leave, what they know is, an oppressive government. The tragic fall of Afghanistan to the Muslim extremists who make up the Taliban was watched by everybody with a smart phone and an internet connection.

All around the world there is fear, and there is terror, and it's trying to take a firm grip and hold of our hearts and our minds. It's trying to control us and prevent us from knowing peace.

And the mainstream media? My word! have they worked overtime to perpetuate the fear of COVID, while stirring the pot of fear and conspiracy theories. We've long left the time when we could turn to the major news sources for neutral coverage of world events.

We've seen fact checkers correcting facts and deleting them, even when they were patently true.

We've seen social media tighten its grip, ensuring that people who are using their platforms only see the worldview they prefer.

It has often been said that you can sell anything, to anybody, if you can show them the need. And the media, and social media, have shown us a need to live in fear and only turn to them for information we can trust. We know we can't, but where else do we turn?

And all of this is going on around us, and maybe it's making you feel emotionally vulnerable, broken, hurt, scared, and alone.

Maybe you've lost loved ones near to you?

Maybe you're living in a situation where you're afraid of COVID, because you know it isn't likely to make you just unwell, but because there is the very real chance of it killing you because of a pre-existing health issue?

Maybe you've lost your business, with no warning? Maybe you've had to tell your staff that you can no longer provide them with the job security that they, and you, took for granted?

Maybe you can no longer feed your family, or your children, or just yourself?

Maybe you're looking ahead to colder weather, knowing that you only really have one choice – buy food or buy fuel?

But how do we respond to that as people?

How should we respond to that as people?

How do we respond to that as Christians?

How should we respond to that as Christians?

Are you hurting inside?

Do you feel alone?

Do you feel raw, emotionally, like you've got nothing left to give?

Do you feel worried about your job, your business, your family, your future?

These are all normal fears that each one of us will have in different ways at different times. But we can be encouraged because Jesus, the Son of God, experienced hard times too, and we can be assured that His burdens were greater than any we will ever have to face.

Chapter 2

'My burden is light?'

Let's read the shortest verse in the Bible together. Because when we're thinking about finding hope, and wondering where to look to find that hope, this verse is rich with spiritual food to warm the soul and lighten the load on our shoulders.

John Chapter 11, verse 35. Just 2 words, and this is what we read:

"Jesus wept."

So, how is this encouraging, and why was Jesus weeping?

Well, someone was dying, and Jesus had gone to see them when He'd been informed, but He had arrived too late. His mourning was a result of the grief He felt because of the death of the person He had gone to see.

The encouraging part, for me - and us - is that Jesus was emotionally distraught. Jesus, the Son of God, has emotions, just like His Father, and just like you and me.

Jesus weeps, and Jesus mourns.

So, when things break our hearts, whether that's people, or situations, or a virus, or war, or the fear of war, we're already in good company. Because Jesus knows more pain than we ever will, which means we all have someone we can go to with those burdens; someone who already knows what we're struggling with.

In my ESV Study Bible [1]it says this:

> *Mourning because of death does not indicate a lack of faith. It shows honest sorrow at the reality of suffering and death.*

And I wonder about our anxiety, our depression, our fear, our worry - that we see ripping through and growing in society, like the most virulent of weeds, or perhaps even a virus.

It is ripping through society, and through our friends, and through our government. It's getting at our hearts, and it's seeking to infect us and control us.

And I think a lot of these struggles we see, and feel, and experience, are the result of the lack of control we feel about them. Because we want to control those scary things around us and keep ourselves safe. And, while it is perfectly

---

[1] ESV® Student Study Bible (Crossway: Good News Publishers, 2011) Page 1416

reasonable, and normal, and natural to want to do so, it is rarely achievable, and certainly not to the degree we would want it to be.

And I think some of that is because we feel like we're supposed to respond to situations in a certain way – that we should be stronger; that we should be weaker; that we should be more vulnerable, more compassionate. And some of these can be good things to strive for. But they can also become weights upon us and become burdens we were never meant to carry, or shoulder the weight of, in the first place.

Jesus' own words remind us that the burden upon us is light, in Matthew 11, verse 30:

> *"For my yoke is easy, and my burden is light."*

So, if you've got a heavy burden, and it's not the one that Jesus wants you to carry, read on and let's find some peace, together.

Chapter 3

'Fear not, for I have redeemed you!'

One of my very favourite pieces of Scripture in the whole of the Bible is Isaiah Chapter 43, verses 1 to 3:

> *"But now thus says the Lord, he who created you, O Jacob, he who formed you, O Israel: 'Fear not, for I have redeemed you; I have called you by name, you are mine. When you pass through the waters, I will be with you; and through the rivers, they shall not overwhelm you; when you walk through fire you shall not be burned, and the flame shall not consume you. For I am the Lord your God, the Holy One of Israel, your Saviour…"*

For me, those words remind me of my coming to faith. It reminds me of that moment, when I was 7 years old, sitting in a large Baptist Church in the West Midlands in the UK, between two loving, faithful, mature, godly people, as I surrendered myself to Jesus Christ, and made Him my Lord and my Saviour.

But I wonder whether, for you, these words create a feeling of comfort, or a feeling of frustration.

God states that, for those of us He calls His own people, He will ensure that we will not be overwhelmed by the fire or the flames. But it certainly doesn't always feel that way, does it?

One of the single greatest mis-taught pieces of Scriptural understanding is that when you come to faith in the Lord Jesus Christ, you will then become problem-free. There is a lie that suggests that you won't have any problems in your life; that everything will be great and rosy; that your life will be wonderful; that you'll never experience problems, or pain, or difficulty, or hardship; that you'll always have all the money you need and experience constant good health. But that is simply not true! It sounds good, and is very alluring, but it doesn't have a shred of truth in it.

While we absolutely do have access to a loving God who heals – I have prayed for people who have been miraculously healed, and I have been miraculously healed myself several times – and, while we will always have everything we could possibly need to accomplish all that God has for us to accomplish, it may well not look like it to us.

Actually, when we choose to follow Jesus, our lives are likely to attract a good deal more negative attention. Which is one reason why we need to make an informed decision to follow Jesus Christ. Becoming a Christian is something Scripture tells us we should think through – it is wonderfully liberating, refreshing, and life changing in the best possible ways, after all.

We need to be fully aware that when we choose to follow Jesus, and become a disciple of Jesus Christ, we also make an enemy of the devil; the moment we choose to follow Jesus Christ, is also the moment we decide not to follow the devil. And the devil doesn't want to lose anybody from his side of the cosmic fence.

As human beings, just like Jesus was (though He was also the Son of God), we don't get to exist outside of life's difficulties, pains, and hurts. We have to walk through them. The key difference, though, is that we will have Jesus Christ to walk through them with us. And that is all the difference in the world!

And what a Man we have to follow! Jesus Christ was born into this world, and His family had to flee for their lives, as refugees, so He wasn't discovered and murdered.

He was betrayed by His closest friends and companions.

His own Father turned His face away when Jesus was on the cross - dying the most horrible death imaginable - for crimes He could not have committed. He allowed Himself to be placed there, in place of people who hated Him and spat at Him.

That is the Man we can choose to follow. And when we keep that in context, alongside a healthy dose of divine perspective, those difficulties we face suddenly appear to disappear. When the Son of God is behind you, you have the greatest supporter you could ever wish for, standing right beside you.

He knows what you're capable of, because He knows His Dad did a good job handcrafting you, for a purpose, and with purpose.

He knows the absolute limits of what the human body can endure in pain and suffering, because He endured more than we will ever have to.

Chapter 4

The well that never runs dry

The Psalms are a great source of encouragement (David's words come from very real, painful experiences), and come with a healthy dose of perspective (not many of us will have to hide in caves, fearing for our lives, while our own King, who really does know better, keeps trying to murder us). They are packed with the largest pearls of wisdom and create, for us, a rhythm of our lives with God. They encourage me because when I am angry at God for failing me, I'm already in good company – and I know that all I need to do is carry on and reinstall God in His proper place in my mind, and in my heart, and in my life.

We find these comforting words in Psalm 34, verse 18, which say this:

"The Lord is near to the broken hearted and saves the crushed in spirit."

This beautifully encouraging piece of Scripture, written by King David, sits within a larger passage that is aimed at people who have chosen to live a life as Followers of the Way; as Christians; as Disciples of Jesus Christ. It is talking specifically to people who love God.

Remembering the words of Isaiah 43 v 1-3 that we read earlier, we see that this is God speaking to His own, chosen, people.

"But now thus says the Lord, he who created you, O Jacob, he who formed you, O Israel: 'Fear not, for I have redeemed you; I have called you by name, you are mine. When you pass through the waters, I will be with you; and through the rivers, they shall not overwhelm you; when you walk through fire you shall not be burned, and the flame shall not consume you. For I am the Lord your God, the Holy One of Israel, your Saviour…"

So, there we have it - God loves us! And that means, of course, that God loves you! But we will still face difficulties and hardships in our lives.

And the truly exciting part of being a Christian is not having to go through life's difficulties alone - it means we don't need to go through life without experiencing anything, or without living a life worth remembering.

It means that we are able to live our lives; we are able to experience everything with the Lord Jesus Christ by our side –

all while knowing that He has gone ahead of us and experienced the very worst versions of everything we will ever have to face.

Consequences Matter!

As Christians, we need to think in terms of consequences.

Without consequences, Jesus' death and resurrection simply mean nothing. It is because of consequences that Jesus allowed Himself to die that death. And it is because of those consequences that Jesus defeated death, because He knew we could not do that. Jesus knew that we couldn't bridge the gap between us and God. So, because of the consequences of doing nothing, Jesus bridged that gap so we can all know the joy of an eternity in heaven, in relationship with our Father God – Jehovah Jireh.

When we think of consequences it's all too easy to jump to memories of being punished for what we've done wrong. Perhaps it makes us remember that speeding ticket we once got, and having to stand in front of a judge, to defend ourselves for our actions.

But consequences don't have to be negative. They are neutral in and of themselves. However, the outcome can be either good or bad.

Get caught speeding? You'll see negative consequences!

Get caught helping someone cross a road? You'll see positive consequences.

Let's come back to that idea of control.

Through the pandemic of COVID-19, we've seen governments seeking to control the people they serve. Sometimes, this has been good, for example, protecting the most vulnerable in our society, by using mask mandates to reduce the spread of airborne particles.

And, sometimes - perhaps more increasingly frequently as the pandemic wore on - those measures of control were obviously nothing to do with protecting the societies they were serving, for example, increasing the ease of access to abortions at home.

Why do I believe I can say this so clearly? Well, because the people setting the rules of lockdowns were so frequently happily, and blatantly, ignoring the rules they were setting. And because there have been so many examples of exemptions - for people who shouldn't have had exemptions - frequently filling news outlets around the world. And when people state one thing, but do another, we can easily know that those things they say are really important, really aren't as important as they'd like us to believe.

Which brings us back to the idea of control, and how that affects our struggles with negative emotions. Because we all want to seek to control our surroundings, to protect ourselves and those we love. And, often, we hope that, by controlling those things which affect us, we may be able to orchestrate a situation which leads to a place where we can be at peace.

But, if you're hurting, and you're broken, and you want to know a peace that isn't affected by your situation, you need to pursue God. Because God is the only true source of that peace - which we are all hungry to pursue.

Chapter 5

Keepin' it real!

As a child, I suffered abuse. I got through that because God was at my side, and by my side.

As a teenager, I struggled in a school system where I just did not fit. I didn't like exams, and I was very uncomfortable there. I was endlessly lonely and afraid.

As a married man, I've had to mourn the loss of our daughter, who tragically died. I've lived through that and come through it.

My wife and I have experienced many of the highs and lows of both good, and horrendously bad, employment. At one point I was in a job where my employer so desperately wanted to destroy me, and my future, that they forced my family into a situation where we had no money; we couldn't pay rent; we couldn't pay for the heating; we couldn't buy food; we couldn't do anything.

It went even further, though, as they were so determined to cause me pain that they tried to destroy any hope of any future employment as well. We became reliant on food banks just to have the ability to provide food for our children.

Why share this with you? Well, it is simply to say that I know what it is like to live through pain and hardship.

And, you might say, "Well, that's great, but that's your life, not mine". But if I've learned nothing else, it is that hurt, hurts. And that pain, is pain. This isn't to belittle your suffering. It is simply to state that I know what it is like to know you can't make it through to the next day. But it is also to state that I know we can!

The Bible tells us, in Ecclesiastes 1, verse 9, that,

> *"What has been is what will be, and what has been done is what will be done, and there is nothing new under the sun."*

And while I may not have been through exactly what you've been through, I've been through enough painful experiences in my life - things nobody should ever have to go through - and I've come through the other side.

And I still know Jesus!

And I still have peace!

And I still have certainty of a hope in my future!

And if you're worried about your future because you feel you don't have one, I can promise you that you do, because the Bible tells me so!

Those experiences of my life, that I mentioned above, are very much a part of my life. They have all defined me, in one way or another. But, while they define me, they don't define all of me.

That childhood abuse led to an adult depression which took 15 months of intense therapy to get past.

Losing a child is one of the most traumatic and singularly painful things I have experienced - knowing that I was utterly helpless to do anything about the fact that my daughter was dying; that she had died; that she was out of my reach to help and protect.

Losing a job? That's pretty hard at any time in life. But losing a job, and knowing that your employer has done everything they can to try and prevent you securing another one, just because they're spiteful and insecure? That is something that keeps you awake at night, makes you lose sleep, and may well put you in hospital with something really bad!

Everything is relative – of course it is! I don't know your pain, any more than you know mine. But I know pain. And I know what it's like to be rejected by people that you're supposed to love, be loved by, and trust, and accept.

But what's really encouraging is the fact that Jesus faced all of this, and much, much more.

One of His closest friends, one of His very closest companions, Judas Iscariot, subjected Jesus to unwarranted misery and pain, by rejecting Him and betraying Him.

As Christians we can say 'yes', that all happened, and that Judas needed to do those things, because we needed that to happen in order to begin what Jesus then went on to do, when He allowed Himself to be hung, to death, on that old, rugged cross.

But, let's not forget the fact that one of Jesus' closest companions and friends rejected Him, abandoned Him, turned on Him, and betrayed Him. Which means that Jesus knew what it was like to suffer pain!

Those painful experiences that we all have to live through - they affect us, don't they? They define part of us, but they don't define all of us!

My daughter dying defines me in certain ways, but it doesn't define everything. We worked through the hurt and pain and sorrow and grief, but we now look back to that time as the moment we decided to start living for today, because we don't know if we'll get another tomorrow. Magdi's life, as short as it was, taught us to embrace life, and live a life worth remembering.

That childhood abuse I had to work through when I was in my 30s? Well, it defined some pretty big parts of me, but it didn't have the power to define all of me. That extremely intensive therapy I went through, for the best part of 18 months? It encouraged my therapist so much – because of how dramatic the positive change in my outlook was – that she went on, with great confidence, to go and help others with similar struggles.

Time doesn't make the pain go away. But with time comes healing, and with healing comes perspective, and with perspective comes strength. And it can all help us depend on Jesus Christ ever more deeply, and relevantly, and actively.

Chapter 6

God's goodness is good!

Jesus was God.

God was Jesus.

Jesus is God.

Jesus lived and worked and walked on Earth.

He was a man.

He knew emotions.

And when we think of the fact that Jesus suffered, it isn't just that He suffered, but He would have suffered more than us. The fact that Jesus was God – His divinity - didn't mean He bypassed pain and suffering. The man bled tears! And that's something I've never yet had to endure; I've never encountered such an extreme emotion.

But Jesus did.

And, actually, I would go further and say that Jesus' divinity didn't protect Him, or help Him avoid pain - it actually allowed Him to feel it even more.

Let's not forget that, whatever else, Jesus, as a man, endured those negatively defining life moments.

He was betrayed by his best friend. He was hated by those He loved. He is still hated by those He loves.

Maybe you've lost a job.

Maybe COVID has made you terrified of going out your front door.

Maybe COVID has changed your world in terrible ways you never thought possible.

Maybe you see what's going on in Afghanistan, and you're terrified that in the UK, or in the US, or somewhere else, that you're going to be attacked on the street in a terrorist attack.

I've also lived through the largest mainland bomb ever detonated in mainland Great Britain – by the IRA - up in Manchester, in the mid-1990s. And my wife-to-be and I, well, let's just say that we were MUCH closer than any news reports would suggest people were…and we came through that too. I had a headache for many weeks, but I was glad that I came off lightly. Others were affected much more severely.

It took me many years to be comfortable in crowded places again, but while that bomb blast, and the following shock wave, defined my wife and I, both physically and emotionally, that 'defining' was both temporary and limited too.

These things, these worries, they can control us and manipulate us, but they don't have to. And certainly not indefinitely.

Let's go back to Psalm 34, verse 18 once more.

"The Lord is near to the broken hearted and saves the crushed in spirit."

Whatever you are going through, God states, in His word - the Bible - that He will be near to you, that He will be near to me.

These aren't just words that sound good. These are God's words, and this is God's promise! It isn't just God spouting off some 'nice thoughts' either. We can guarantee that God will follow through on what He says. He is the One we can truly trust. Failing us simply isn't in His nature.

Let's circle back to some of those consequences we face in life.

We live in a fallen world. And some of the consequences of the fallen world are death, and illness, and sickness. As disciples of Jesus, as said above, we're not going to be able to avoid that. Those difficulties, those sufferings? They're a part of life!

But one of the consequences of this life is that we try and control the situation around us, in order to protect ourselves from further hurt or pain.

And what does that do? Well, ultimately, it will create loneliness, because we'll build so many barriers around us that no one will ever get near us. And, while putting up some healthy barriers around us can be good for a time – to protect ourselves or to heal – we also need to eventually remove those barriers. Because, as people, we are designed and created by God to interact with other human beings.

But in life we're often guilty of trying to control the pain and the misery around us. We think that if we can control enough of those issues, they won't then be able to affect us. Or at least we hope they will be sufficiently, drastically, reduced.

Those things that can keep us awake at night might be:

Will I get fat when I get older?

Will I not be able to walk?

Will I get dementia?

Will I struggle with this disease, or with that physical disability?

Will I lose my job when I'm 58, and be unable to ever get meaningful employment again?

These are things that can easily keep us awake at night, whether we know Jesus or not! And as we go through life there are, of course, different phases and seasons - when we try and control what's going on around us.

Perhaps you're doing yoga, or reflexology, or you're into finding anything where you hope you will be able to create some peace in your life.

Maybe you go out drinking every evening, and you sleep with somebody different every night, because you're desperately trying to find someone who will show you love and acceptance, but in such a way that leaves you in control, and creates opportunities to, maybe, experience peace somewhere.

Maybe drug-taking is something you're struggling with. And perhaps your particular drug of choice is your work - you work so hard for financial security, because you hope that you'll create enough of a buffer so that you'll be financially okay as you get older, in order that that might provide some peace later on.

But money can be stolen, or lost, or disappear. And we saw, tragically, here in the UK, how many people had been paying into particular pension providers, over their working lifetime – to provide financial security when they retired – only to see that money disappear before they could access it.

Money is not a guarantee of peace! And neither is marriage. Friends can be great, but they can't secure you peace either. Working to hold a secure job, or having the most senior position in a job. None of these things are going to give us peace - only the illusion of an uncertain peace.

There's nothing wrong with working hard. The Bible tells us we should work a 6 day week, and work hard when there is daylight.

And there's nothing wrong with seeking to improve the life around you - Jesus had 12 companions with whom He spent much of His time while in Ministry.

But there is something wrong with doing all these things for our own gain, and not doing them for others. As Christians, we're supposed to be a part of building God's Kingdom, and not building our own kingdoms.

We have to acknowledge the simple truth that we cannot control the people around us that are hurting us. We can't totally prevent them from doing that. We can do all sorts of things to try and limit it, and sometimes that's wise and that's right, but people will still hurt us. And sometimes it doesn't even have anything to do with us.

Just Breathe

Often, suffering comes along in ever increasing waves, doesn't it? Those times when you're utterly devastated and broken emotionally, financially, physically, and mentally.

You think 'Okay, God, nothing else - I can't cope with anything else happening to me.'

And then you have a flood in your house.

And then the washing machine breaks down.

And then the food that you bought with the last of your money? Well, that's in the freezer with the broken door that doesn't close, which was left open overnight, and stopped working the day before.

And life can get progressively worse, and worse, and worse, and worse, until you feel and think that you won't be able to breathe.

And as a family, that isn't just dramatic and interesting to read – that's the life we've been through, personally. And it sucked at our very last breath to keep breathing!

We've been at the end of ourselves financially.

We've been at the end of ourselves emotionally.

We've been at the end of ourselves mentally.

But the one thing we've never lost sight of is the fact that God loves us and provides for us. He's never let us experience more than He was willing to help us through.

Chapter 7

Peace, like a warm blanket

If you're suffering, or if you're feeling broken, or if you're feeling like your situation is unique to you, and that no one is going to understand your problem, then we need to look a little at how the devil works. Because the devil is a very real opponent.

One of the most productive techniques I've seen the devil use, that I've observed in other people, and my own life, is to make us feel like we're the only person dealing with a particular issue.

The Bible tells me, clearly, that that simply is not true! Because there are many people struggling with lots of things.

Comparing our pain to them is a fruitless and soul-destroying exercise! We are all unique, and we have all experienced different pains and struggles. So, two people dealing with the exact same issue will be able to cope differently, because of their previous experiences; because of their character; because of how much sleep they've been getting; because of the quality of their food; because of how balanced their hormones are! It all effects how we deal with life's difficulties.

And as a man who has walked this earth for well into 4 decades, I'm ever more certain that whatever problem I'm facing, somebody has faced it in the last few thousand years too – I am unique, but I am not alone!

The devil always loves to use the magnifying glass of history and fear to make something seem far bigger than it is – to make a problem seem more insurmountable than it ever could be in our own imagination.

The Early Years

When my wife and I were planning to get married, we were told that "everyone's against you getting married, everybody; it's bad, it's just terrible, don't do it!" Even on our wedding day people felt the need to keep repeating how horrible we were for getting married, and how stupid and pointless it all was.

However, when we actually counted up the people who were indeed opposed to us getting married? Yeah, there were a few louder voices that were making the noise and grumblings. But you know what? Everybody else we met was very much in favour of us getting married. But, because a few people who mattered to us said that everyone was against it, we believed those lies.

Loud voices can scream for attention. And truth always suffers when perception seems to scream louder! But it's so easy to listen to the lies, isn't it? Because they sometimes seem more true than the truth. It's a frustrating, interesting paradox, isn't it?

But if you want to know peace, it isn't just a case of being near to God, and then you'll know peace, and then all's good. It isn't just a question of 'here's the formula, off you go' and then you'll finally know that peace you've been after, either.

Chapter 8

Footprints, and guarantees

Let's come back to control and consequences, just one more time.

We want to control the world around us, to protect ourselves from being hurt, by creating ourselves as secure and as firm a foundation as we can, so that it will be all good because then, nothing's gonna be able to hurt us. We've watched other people, looked at how bad they've lived their lives, and then we realise that actually that's just us - trying to manipulate and control the situation around us - and it doesn't actually give us the peace we were hoping for.

Because, if you want to know peace, there are a few things that you need to do.

The first and most important? You need a relationship with the Lord Jesus Christ!

But it's not just a relationship where you know OF Jesus Christ. Because you need to KNOW Jesus Christ - in the most real ways possible. You need to know Him as your Lord and Saviour. You need to be a disciple of Jesus Christ and follow Him. You need to repent of, or say sorry for, those things in your life that you know are not as good as you pretend they are.

And it isn't to say that if you don't know Jesus Christ, then you'll never know any peace. That's not what we're talking about here.

But if you want to know, and live with, a peace that transcends and goes beyond all human understanding, and experience defining life moments, then you need to have a relationship WITH Jesus Christ. And we need the Holy Spirit to help us through our lives as we change from who we were, to the men and women God purposefully made us to become during our lives.

It simply isn't enough to just go through life, and try and protect ourselves from hurt and harm. We need to understand what the devil is doing, not by focusing on him, but by realising that all the stuff that we're struggling with - that we're thinking we're alone in our suffering with - others are gonna be struggling with similar stuff too.

And as sure as eggs are eggs, somebody else is struggling with the same things you are.

So, how do we defeat the lies that seek to crowd our thoughts?

Well, really simply, you get into the Living Word; you get into the Bible; you read Scripture; you pray; you spend time with other Christians - you spend time deliberately focusing on the Lord Jesus Christ.

Philippians 4, verse 8, reminds us to 'focus on whatever is good and pure and lovely':

> *"Finally, brothers, whatever is true, whatever is honourable, whatever is just, whatever is pure, whatever is lovely, whatever is commendable, if there is any excellence, if there is anything worthy of praise, think about these things."*

And Romans 5, verses 1 to 5, says this - in the passage, wonderfully titled in my Bible, Peace with God Through Faith:

> *"Therefore, since we have been justified by faith, we have peace with God through our Lord Jesus Christ. Through him we have also obtained access by faith into this grace in which we stand, and we rejoice in hope of the glory of God. Not only that, but we rejoice in our sufferings, knowing that suffering produces endurance, and endurance produces character, and character produces hope, and hope does not put us to shame, because God's love has been poured into our hearts through the Holy Spirit who has been given to us."*

That difficulty in your life? The one which you think you're never going to get beyond? You can get past it and through it!

But don't just pray to God to get it *out* of your way, or for Him take you around it. Pray to God, that He will be with you as you walk *through* that situation.

Remember those words from Isaiah 43, verse 2?

> *"When you pass through the waters, I will be with you; and through the rivers, they shall not overwhelm you; when you walk through fire you shall not be burned, and the flame shall not consume you."*

It doesn't say that when we pass *by* the waters that God will be with us.

It doesn't say that when we *see* flames from afar, that God will be with us.

It tells us that *in the midst of the storm*, at *that* point, God will be with us.

We can, and will always try to, bypass pain. But it never fully works. We can try and think that we're the only ones that are dealing with this, but that isn't true! The reality is that we all suffer, and we have all fallen short of the glory of God.

We all have difficulties and struggles in our life that we have to face, often on our own. But Jesus Christ is not just there for the good times in our lives - He's there for both the good times AND the bad times.

He is always there, if we choose to let Him walk alongside us. And He can always walk alongside us, because He's walked ahead of us, and knows those paths we tread along.

Chapter 9

'Character produces hope'

Let's take a look at those comforting words we read in Romans 5.

"Not only that, but we rejoice in our sufferings..."

This definitely doesn't mean that we're supposed to be happy about the bad things we face in life, but that we can choose to rejoice because Jesus Christ is walking with us through those trials and sufferings.

"...knowing that suffering produces endurance..."

We can be assured that our suffering is not pointless – that hardship is not a waste of time – but it can also be an opportunity for you and me to get closer to Jesus Christ, as

He helps us get through those difficulties, producing endurance in us.

"…suffering produces endurance…"

And this means we can keep going, even beyond the point at which we think we're done in!

"…endurance produces character…"

Character is so important! We all want it. We all prefer people who have a pleasant character. And if we want to improve our own character, how do we achieve that?

Well, going back to Romans 5, we see that character comes from endurance, and endurance comes from suffering. Which means it doesn't have to be pointless suffering, because all can work for our good, and for the Kingdom of God.

Do you want to work on your character? Have you been praying for God to help you be a better person, with a better character?

Then you're gonna probably get some difficult stuff in your life, that you'd rather go around. But if you go around it, rather than through it, remembering those words from Isaiah 43 – that God will be there with us – then you'll miss out on the opportunity to become more like Jesus; you'll miss out on the opportunities to be refined.

And every process of refining I can think of that is referred to in the Bible is the less gentle type – like refining gold…there ain't nothing gentle about that process! But, that process produces one of the most precious, and sought after, materials in the world. And who doesn't want to be seen like that gold? But, the consequence of becoming that precious metal, is that we need to be willing to undergo various processes to get there.

"…character produces hope…"

If you want to know hope, to bring hope, to live hope - in a hopeless world - you need character. And how do we 'get' character? Well, character comes from endurance.

Where does the endurance come from? Endurance comes from suffering!.

And what's suffering got to do with it? Well, for everything that's happening to us, we can rejoice that Jesus Christ is with us, and that He can turn everything we go through into the most precious of precious metals.

Don't ever rejoice that you're struggling with unemployment, or the fact you can't feed your children. That's simply not something to be glad of, or to rejoice in. But we can rejoice because we know that Jesus Christ is with us. And, we can rejoice because Jesus Christ will walk alongside us.

I know the pain and struggle of not being able to feed my children. I've been there, more than once! But I also know what it's like to rejoice in the hope that God has got this and see what God's plan was to make that ordeal into something far better.

If you're struggling with emotional turmoil, anxiety, depression, and fear. If all these things, and more besides, are trying to get to your heart. Then there is a solution.

And that solution is called Jesus Christ. It's called having a relationship with Jesus Christ.

Chapter 10

Who's driving again?

We can either move towards Jesus Christ, or we can move away from Him. There is no standing still.

Somebody once did a study of the Old Testament prophets and said that they would have been very susceptible to depression. If you're THAT close to God, and being toe to toe with God, and then you move away - so you're not so very close to Him - then you're gonna feel a huge movement from being close to God, and far away from God. That movement to and from God is what somebody believed the prophets would have gone through.

But what a great illustration it is, also, of why we need to be constantly making efforts to be moving towards God.

As we get closer towards God, we're going to want to get closer again. But, getting closer to God, and becoming more like Jesus Christ, means losing some of the 'us' from us, so that we can become more like Jesus Christ.

As we get closer to Jesus Christ, we want to be more like Him, which means surrendering those parts of us that we want to hang on to, and control - because life tells us that it's those things that are keeping us safe, and that they make us OK.

But when we surrender those things - that we see as ridiculously important to our very survival - to Jesus Christ, we find ourselves no longer with clenched fists hanging on tightly, and we realise that those things we've been hanging on to, really aren't as important as we had allowed them to become in our minds.

Let me paint a picture for you of how we often move along through life.

Imagine you've already made the decision to let Jesus sit in in the driving seat of your car.

And He's driving along.

And you're there.

And you remember that you've trusted Him to sit in the driving seat of your life because, you know, He is a really good driver, with better than 20/20 vision, and the reactions that are exceptionally faster than the very best test pilot.

And He's got his hands on the steering wheel.

And He's there, and He's driving along, quite relaxed.

And you sit there, letting Him do the gear changes.

And you let Him look after the hand brake, and the accelerator.

But you've also installed a second brake pedal, on your side of the car.

And you've also got your hand on the steering wheel, just in case Jesus doesn't notice that thing down the road, that might be dangerous, that He should have already started slowing down for and avoiding.

And you've got your foot covering that brake pedal, just in case He forgets where it is, or if He starts going faster than you know your car can safely travel without you in the driving seat.

If we want to know what it is to be peaceful, then we need to take our hands off that steering wheel, take out the second brake pedal that we installed, stop worrying about Jesus' ability to see what we can plainly see is a threat just ahead (that we've already surrendered to Jesus Christ, but wonder if He remembers we gave to Him) and let the Master Driver steer us along the roads He's already travelled many times before.

Did I mention He's also a Master Navigator with a photographic memory?

As we trust in Jesus Christ to guide our life, through the power of the Holy Spirit, it is then that we can truly know that sweet, life-altering, heart-calming peace. That peace that transcends all understanding, and goes so far beyond our human comprehension, that we know we can't understand, but is so very real!

Chapter 11

The path, well travelled, and well known

If you want to know hope, because you feel hope has left you, or if you feel that hope is, now, so far away from you that you're just never going to know it again - let's rejoice in our suffering.

And just to say this one more time: we don't rejoice that bad stuff is happening to us, or to those we love. Because that is absolutely *not* rejoicing in your suffering. Rejoicing in your suffering is knowing that Jesus Christ is walking alongside you, and that whatever difficulty you are going through, as Corrie Ten Boom wonderfully said, is Jesus preparing you for heaven. And that's worth rejoicing in!

And let us allow to sink into our hearts the fact that:

"Suffering produces endurance. Endurance produces character. Character produces hope. And [that] hope does not put us to shame."

If you want to know peace; if you're struggling with anxiety, I wonder if you would value saying the prayer that follows.

Because one of the first parts of gaining access to the peace I'm describing requires that we, first, surrender, our lives to God.

Maybe this is something you've never done before. And maybe this isn't your first time asking God to accept you as His own.

Perhaps you've been going great guns for God, but, you think He forgot about that pain you went through, and you let distance increasingly come between you and the God who loves you, and cares deeply for you – the God who hand made you with purpose, and on purpose, and who let His own Son die, so that none of us would have to.

Can I ask you to let that hurt go and make yourself right with God once again?

And if you don't know Jesus at all, and you've been reading this, I want you to know the peace that I've known, that my family has known through some emotionally crippling moments – the kind that make 'white knuckling it' sound like a pleasure cruise.

When I was being abused as a child; when I was losing my daughter and she died; when I was having to go to the Food Bank because I couldn't afford to feed my children; when people were circling our family, trying to attack us and prevent us from being ever able to work again, I knew God's peace.

And that's the peace I would love you to be able to experience, no matter what your suffering has been, or is right now. Because I want you to be able to rejoice in those sufferings as we did. Not happy that they're happening to you, but rejoicing because we know that God is very much with us, and behind us, and by us, and all around us.

There is a piece of Scripture that has carried me through some pretty dark moments - 2 Corinthians 12:10.

> *"That is why, for Christ's sake, I delight in weaknesses, in insults, in hardships, in persecutions, in difficulties. For when I am weak, then I am strong."*

I used to mis-hear that as 'when we are weak, then we are strong'.

But the true beauty of this Scripture, is that when we are weak, then He is strong, *in* us.

And if I'm going to amplify that a little bit with my own words it would read a little like this: when you're in a difficulty; when something's really got you down on the floor, and you feel like you're never going to get up again, it's because of that weakness, when we surrender ourselves to Jesus Christ, and because of that weakness, that God is then able to comfort us and help us.

If you want to do so, let's pray to God, shall we – using the prayer on the next page?

Let us pray

Heavenly Father, we thank you that you love us. We thank you, God, that you sent your son, Jesus, to die on the cross for me.

Thank you, Jesus, that you died on the cross for me, that you carried the pain, and the suffering, and all the hurt and lies that were upon you, and all the hatred that was upon you, and you endured that, because you loved me, because you still love me, and because you will still, ongoingly, love me.

Lord, I'm sorry for those times when I've turned my face away from you - when I've let my arrogance and my pride get in the way, and when I've tried to face life on my own, knowing I can't do it, but try to anyway.

Forgive me God when I've not surrendered the control of my life to you, that I know you are longing to relieve me of - if I surrender it to you.

Father, would you forgive me of my sins of the past? Would you forgive me of those things that I've done wrong against other people, and against you?

Would you forgive me of those times when I've denied you? Because I want to follow you! I want to make you my Lord and Saviour, from this point forwards.

Father God, I choose, right now, to follow you, and let you steer my life along the paths that I know, you know, better than me.

I choose, at this point, to surrender the pain in my life, to you, knowing that I can rejoice in my suffering, because suffering produces character, character produces endurance, and endurance produces hope. And a hope in you is worth having.

Thank you for the freedom I know I now have, and the feeling of peace I can enjoy. Fill me with the power of your Holy Spirit so I can learn to grow in you, through the Bible, and as I pray to you.

Amen!

If you've said that prayer, and it's the first time you've ever prayed that; if it's the first time you've wanted to let go of your past, and make Jesus your Lord and Saviour - would you get in touch with your local church, or with people who you know who love Jesus?

A good starting point could be the website - www.the4points.com - which explains, further, what a life with Jesus is all about; what it means; why it matters.

Used by permission the4points.com

You can get in touch with us via our website - www.berrybunch.family. You'll find a wide range of resources – posts, videos and more – which you can share, stream and download at your leisure.

Fire up your faith, with the BerryBunch: for free, for all!

And, one more brilliant resource - which we use very frequently - is Bible Gateway[2]. If you don't own your own

---

[2] Bible Gateway - https://www.biblegateway.com/

bible, or simply would prefer to read Scripture in different ways, it is a wonderful place to spend some time!

And, along with Bible Gateway, another great, and similarly free, resource is an APP by You Version[3]. It allows you to download versions of the bible, in full - and in your own language, and in a style that you find most helpful – right on to your smartphone or tablet.

If you've decided that you want to follow God because you've just not been taking it seriously, and you've let this particular hurt, or worry, or pain, or problem become bigger than your trust in Jesus Christ, just let it go and tell God how you feel, knowing that He absolutely WILL catch you.

He may not catch you in the way you want. But it is SO worth it!

When we didn't have food for our children, and we were praying at God's door for money to come through the letterbox - so we could go out and buy food – it didn't happen.

But what did happen was even better, because somebody referred us to a food bank and we got to meet some lovely people, who we otherwise wouldn't have met. That wasn't our plan – but it was God's!

Our plan was to be given the money, retain our pride, and go and buy food ourselves. But, actually, the kindness - and that

---

[3] YouVersion - https://youversion.com/

interaction with those people at the food bank - was a really precious moment. And we wouldn't have had that compassionate care, if we hadn't been through those difficulties. And we wouldn't have gained such a great understanding of what it's like to be unemployed, unable to get a job, unable to feed our own children, and unable to buy fuel to heat our home.

I'm not saying I'm happy about all those things happening! But, because they happened, we developed and deepened our relationship with God, and we trust Him even more. That closeness to God that we felt, directly because of those difficult times, are beyond precious, even now, many years on.

Through life we are either moving towards God, or we're moving away from Him. There's no middle ground! You can't stand still! That's not a choice! You choose to move towards God, or you choose to move away.

So, let's choose to move towards God. And let's choose to move towards that peace. And let's choose to work with, and through the pain and hurts of life on our own.

So let go of the hurts, and let Jesus know about them.

He already does anyway! And He's walked the paths ahead of you, and He won't ever fail you.

Printed in Poland
by Amazon Fulfillment
Poland Sp. z o.o., Wrocław

88286833R00038